Into

the Thorns and Honey

Poems and Photos
by Glenn Bowie

ISBN: 978-0-9965405-4-4

Printed in the United States of America

Front Cover Photo: Glenn Bowie
Back Cover Photo: Jennifer Matthews

Also by Glenn Bowie
Under the Weight of Whispers

BIG TABLE Publishing

Big Table Publishing Company
Boston, MA
www.bigtablepublishing.com

Acknowledgements

I'd like to thank everyone who mapped out my journey with the smallest of things, the love binding it all together, my family who I love very much, and all my friends that have shared in this journey.

I'd like to thank: my sweet wife Joy, and my two children Andrew and Scott who make me so proud; Robin Stratton, without whom this book would not exist–her friendship above all else is what defines her; Rose Boghos, who reached into my soul and pulled out the writer within me; Jennifer Matthews, a brilliant artist and friend who has taught me how to capture light through my lens and through my life– she is a light filled with love and I am grateful that we met; Sue Leonard, who believed in my words from the very beginning–she is like a sister to me; Cindy Dell and Brenny Burns (Leonard , Burns and Dell) who let me share in their musical path; Lizanne Knott, who has been such a wonderfully caring soul–we have found our way to a beautiful friendship; Jeff Black , one of my favorite singer-songwriters, who reached out to me.

Also thanks go to some people I feel I've known forever: Doug Holder, a brilliant writer and warm soul who gives selflessly so that others may flourish; Chelle Rose, a true, kind heart; Chuck Leah–we have yet to meet, but he has been a friend and brother who is an amazing artist; Hank Beukema for his belief in my words and all his efforts to share my work with the world; Michael Caruso, who has had my back from the beginning; and all my friends and fellow musicians, poets and photographers: Simon Paradis, Brian Hazelbower, Ian (Fingers) McMillan, Lucy LeBlanc, Julie Schimunek, Lucinda D Ackland, Nathan T Senner, Andi and Ren Renfree, Amanda Pearcy, Elvin Berthiaume, Rich Briere, Pam Edgar, Luanie Kologi (Blue), Cary Cooper, Richard Fox, Tony Press, Jason Fisk, Paul Beckman, Buck Wilcox, Jo Ann Hanstrom, James Patrick Rafuse, Ricky McCoy, M. Glenn Mitchell, Dario Saraceno, Morghan Brookens, Chris Monk

Seely, Erin McFadden, Nara Elizabeth Farrell, and Howard Michael Paul and his dog Rikki.

Lots of love and gratitude to my mother, who has been a rock for the entire family for so many years, and to all my Facebook friends and followers.

If I've forgotten anyone, I apologize–but you all know that I love you very much.

Peace , G

Table of Contents

Silent Poetry

There's a poetry to the silence
a space where there are no words
a place that you can contemplate
think about everything that was ever said
or nothing at all
there's a poetry to the silence

Two Feathers

She held two feathers in her hands
that had fallen from beyond the stars
as if time and her mind would one day understand
their calling

She knew that peace of mind was where the chords fell
from her blue guitar
landing in the spaces inside his heart
it was so beautiful to his ears to hear
her music falling

He held love in his hands
it flowed from the tips of his fingers
like two feathers
it was flying every time he touched her skin
as if time and his mind would one day understand
why he was always falling
why her kiss
lingered on his lips
when it was only a split second in time
still it was where the spark of two hearts
begins
like where love slips from his pen
dripping with rhyme

She held two feathers in her hands
one for her heart
one for his heart
they would fly as one someday
as if time and their minds knew the place love starts

She held two feathers in her hands
destiny knows only one direction
to play out as planned
She held two feathers in her hands
that had fallen
from beyond the stars
two feathers that always knew
exactly
where to land

Sanctuary

And the old tree said to the tiny bird

I will always let you rest safely in my arms
I will never refuse you
I will grip this violent earth so tightly
Let you make my limbs your home
I am grounded

I ask of you only one condition
that you sit in my arms and sing

sing
as if you've flown this wide world looking for shelter

sing
as if it is in these branches that touch the clouds
gathering the sun
you've found a peace

sing
as if you've flown this great earth looking for sanctuary
and here in my arms
you have finally found it

A Memory Less Traveled

I'm searching for a memory less traveled
a dusty back road in my mind
I never took the time to see where it could go
signposts of regret pointing the way back
to another time as my life now unravels

I'm searching for a memory less traveled
that I left so far behind
Searching again for that common thread
common ground
a stitch in time that came unwound
Things we once said sit silently now
trying so hard not to make a sound

I'm searching for the memory less traveled
the curtains that were drawn as we moved on
everything we touched once now leveled
there's still a path overgrown with regret
a photograph that captured love

a love I'll never forget

Perfect Rain

There are days that sink below
the heart line
Days that will always rise above

There are days that lie quietly along
the heart line
The ones you will never forget

It was a perfect rain
where every raindrop fell
into place
It was a perfect rain
from the heavens of love

As perfect as the day we met
beautiful hours that bloomed like flowers
We watched them grow along
the heart line

in a trace of a moment

A Curve

There's a curve to the moon's light
Rivers bend and wash the earth
Waters that only the sea can divide
The sky, so forgiving and blue
The tide is like a heartbeat
A murmur that time never knew

There is a Devil that lives under your skin,
an Angel on your breath that knows nothing but sin

A tower of dreams you've built with one stone
I'll take it all down with one wave of my hand
Follow the days back to a time, reclaim my throne

The dusk is written off as a shadow that has fallen behind your heart
You see with your hands, your touch , it slowly tears me apart

There's a curve to the light inside your soul
You deliver the ending before I can begin
For what it's worth
This tale's been told

Something as brave as a diamond you wear on one finger
You let time in, whispering to it softly, don't linger
You whisper to time, *Don't ever linger*

All the Pieces of Me

It's blue where you used to stand inside my heart
I miss the you that was in love with me
They say if love won't save you it'll tear you apart

Kiss me goodbye now
all the pieces of me

I don't have to tell you the way the rain will fall
or which way the wind will blow
I will only tell you what needs to be
and that I miss the you that was in love with me

Inner Peace

Who knew that my inner peace
        I would find inside of you
You shake your coat from your shoulders
        like it's a second skin
Whispering
        this is where the ends meet
        this is where love begins

You say you'll never forgive time
        for all the years it kept us apart
All the years you had slept outside on the doorstep
        of my heart

Time will always move along
        you're here now
Inside gravity's pull, where the ends meet, feet planted firmly
        where you belong

Happiness will never be handed to us.
It will always be a pursuit.

Five Hundred and Forty Nine

Untie this heart from the dock and let me drift
aimlessly
Stop the hands of every single clock
tie them behind the world's back
indefinitely
Hang a prayer of light upon the wind
set my sails for what it's worth

Let my time on Earth
begin
the endgame is always Heaven, the one true
North

Test the waters for any sin, I'm
floating
on a beautiful whim, my heart so
deep

There's an undercurrent of love,
an undertow
I will pull you under my world of wonder
drown you

Set my sails, I'm waiting on the winds of
Valhalla
Blow open the five hundred and forty nine doors into
our dreams

Aloneness

An hour or two late, it's not the same
when no one's waiting
You turn the key and it's so quiet you hear the tumblers
like the rumble of thunder
Your mind debating ,

> *Do I turn back the key*
> *lock the door and walk away?*

The little voice inside your head
never knows the right things to say
All alone one more night
on top of one more night
someone could come and save you with a thing called
> *love.*

You'll dream of this long after you turn out the lights
The tapping of the rain on the windows
always the same no matter which way the wind blows
Like a kettle drum
You settle for some kind of compromised peace of mind

The clock on the wall won't even give you the time
one more day, on top of one more day
The little voice inside your head
never knows the right thing to say
An hour or two late, it's not the same
when no one's home

The years in between, few and far
it's where you are
a place you call
all alone

Insomnia

Sunlight so wide and deep
carry me to another nighttime
where I might find some rest
upon the shores of sleep

Wind so wild and possessive
carry me into the arms of Love's limbs
where I can begin to uncoil
into sleep so blessed

Night so wide and dark
it's where I keep my heart in the shadows of forever
where my dreams so elusive and clever
climb a mountain of wishes

There is a magic to the night
where the absence of the light brings my dreams
to the surface
There is a river that flows
where consciousness knows its true purpose

Dreams so steep they free fall into the other side
where peace resides upon the shores
of sleep

Home Once

You touched the wheels of a train, you told me
because it rolled across the countryside
Drank a bottle full of rain
because it was something you said belonged to the sky
You held me in your arms once
because you said that I was love
pure love
inside

You touched the bottom of the ocean, you told me
because it holds all the water upon this blue Earth
You touched the wing of an eagle and the heart of an Angel
because you said we both could fly
You held me in your arms once
because you said you were home there
in my
arms

Jaded

There is a song I heard tomorrow
written with words you never said
a heart that someone borrowed
the truth it never bled
a promise you made to the stars
as jealous as jade
a place where no soul will ever tread
I can only stand in one corner of your heart
I'll never ask you what you dream
fire is something you learn not to touch
as desperate as this seems

There is a promise you made to the stars
angels they are as envious as jade
time has missed a step
through an ocean now of forever
you must wade
there is a song I heard tomorrow
written with words you wish you'd said
in your heart
you cup the sorrow and pray
it leads us somewhere
somewhere
where tears
are never shed

Blacktop Pockets

Keep the road in your pocket
                  for a quick getaway
Don't ever fall in love
                    it's easier that way

When it comes time to leave
                  kiss them only on the cheek
When it comes time to say goodbye
                  count the words that you speak

Keep the motor running
                  never put your heart in park
Turn on the light of the sun
                  when they try to get close in the dark

When it comes time to leave
                  when it comes time to go
You won't have to untangle your heart
                  it'll hang by a thread, but you'll know

Keep the road in your pocket
                  Keep your sun in the sky
And when you have to leave
                  no one will need to cry

                  And no one will ever ask

My Sky

My sky stagnant with forgotten stars
they all weep with jealousy
for a sun that revolves around you
hanging in my heart a sign
forgotten like the stars
it bleeds the words
I still love you

Someone else's sky
Someone else's tears
The sun will shine tomorrow
The stars will all disappear
Someone else's dreams
Someone else's heart
A sky that falls in a million pieces
It's my sky
as I watch it all fall apart

The sun will shine on everyone
You just have to know where to stand
Why is it my forever always hangs
in someone else's hands

The sun and moon they share your stage
You always outshine them all
They can't compete with a heart that shines so bright
You pick the stars you want to fall
Someone else's whispers
Someone else's sky
so far above my world
I can't turn and say goodbye

Some dreams won't let me sleep
My heart won't let me shed this skin
so I close my eyes anyway
waiting on something to begin
Someone else's love
surrounds your heart and hangs your stars
forgotten stars that shine upon my world
Someone else now inside your heart

 Someone else's promises
Someone else's destiny
The stars set in place like jewels
They all begin to fall
so slow, so deliberately
The sky begins to fall in a million pieces
It's my sky

The only thing left that belongs to me

The prayer you spoke to me turned the tide
I saw the backs of the leaves
like a storm wind turns them around

Ghost

Someone once told me
(I believe it was your ghost in my sleep)
that there are things that will always leave us
the things we need the most
the things we love the most
the things we aren't allowed to keep

Like This

She tucks the red Sunset under her pillow
says goodnight to the moon and the stars
through a curtain filtered window
arches her back like a warm southern wind would
bend a willow pretending her hands are his
touches herself in a place
that only he would come to know

She pretends her fingers are his
she whispers as if he were here
touch me baby
like this
like only you know how
you'll be here soon
I'll make it through this lonely night
somehow

She sings a song she wrote herself
kisses his picture twice
pretends her fingers are his
She whispers
kiss me baby
touch me baby
like this, baby
just like this

It's another long night of twisted sheets
his voice on the phone was so
honey sweet
she knows that voice is from the lips
she longs to kiss
nothing in her life has ever felt so right

she whispers quietly
to the wanton night
you'll be here soon
to hold me tight
I'm counting the days
and the starry nights
there's no one else
I'll ever miss

She arches her back like a warm southern wind would
bend a willow, pretending her hands are his
she touches herself in a place
that only he is allowed to go

She places her hand upon her heart
where only he is allowed to touch
where only he is
allowed
to go

I Woke Too Soon

I carved a heart out of wood
        painted it red
        wrote on it some words
        you once said

I carved some truth out of bone
        stood it alone
        against the test of time
        it didn't rhyme

I woke too soon
        followed a dream within
        called your name
        it wasn't the same

Spinning Moon

Spinning Moon shining
half as much as the sun
do you know what it means
to miss someone
do you know what it means
to cry

Just Be You

She said

> what would you do if you woke each morning
> and the mist arose like dew
> if the flowers spoke to the sun
> with each day brand new

She said

> what would you do if the Earth kept turning
> fires of the stars kept burning
> trees reached for a better view
> what would you do

Then she smiled
She kissed my lips and
She said

> don't do anything
> just be you
> just be you

If ever there was a place that felt like home
it would be reading between the white lines out on the road

Weight of Whispers

You'll never be one to break
under the weight of love
whispering prayers of somedays and somewheres
that you have dreamed of

I'll be the one who whispers
the word "forever" in your ear
making true on the promises
you wished for someday and somewhere

I'll touch a finger to your lips
as heartaches disappear
Ghosts are words you never said
that's why they reappear

Someday, somewhere
It's all coming clear
I will find you here

under the weight of whispers

Whisper your dreams to me
and I will make them come true
Your heart's a sweet melody
and I will sing it back to you

Time was an afterthought that you forgot
while I was waiting
perhaps you thought my promises were not
worth debating

Someday, somewhere
It's all coming clear
I will find you here

under the weight of whispers

Last Train

I may be gone from view
I may be out of sight
but I'll still hang the moon
outside your window tonight

The last train down these tracks tonight
as I stand here in the station
is the one I call *don't look back*
the one I call *no hesitation*

I may be gone from view
I may be out of sight
but I'll still hang the moon
like a little nightlight

Look up before you close your eyes
You'll see the moon tonight
hold fast to your dreams
I'll leave a star shining bright

Words

You fill the sky with lightning
     and breathe a word like beautiful
     from your crooked lungs

You fill the books with words
     and hang them in the sky
     where before only broken clouds

     like abstract paintings
     hung

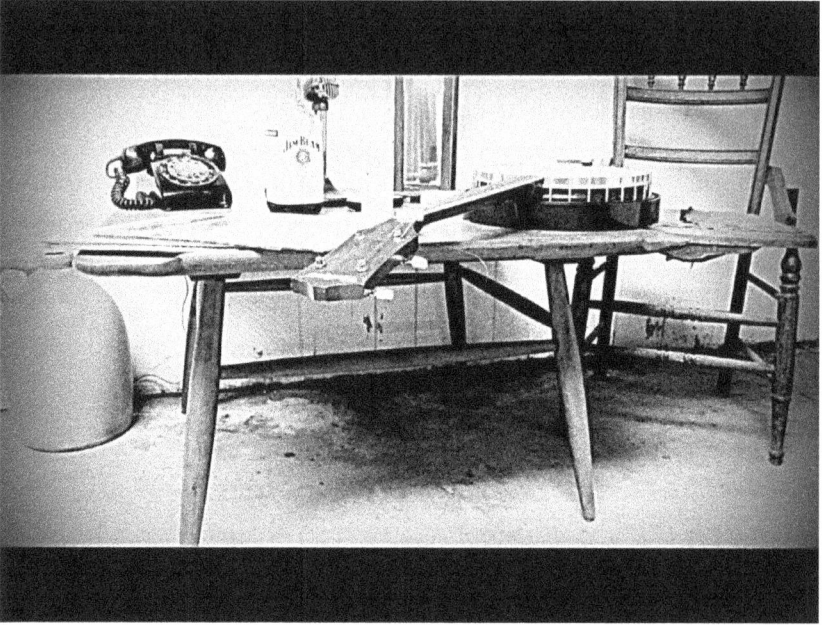

I feel like I'm always chasing something
and when you chase something
it runs away.

Breath

The Ocean held its breath like the waves of the sky
held its breath till it turned blue
I've dreamed about you enough to know that love
in my eyes is every part
starting with the heart
of you

You took one of my whispers I gave you
folded it in half
like a beautiful photograph
held your breath
placed it in the corner of your heart
that once turned blue

The World learned how to turn from watching you
the wind held its breath
then it blew, watching snowflakes follow in hot pursuit
melting when they touched you

I've dreamed of you enough to know that love
starting with your heart
is every part
of you

A Song on the Radio

You heard a song on the radio
no one else heard
it flew around your head
like a beautiful fledgling bird

It wrapped around your heart
sent you flying
that's why when it ended it left
you crying

Once you believed you could fly
you could spin your spirit to the sky

You heard a song on the radio
it asked your heart why
no one ever knew
why you cry

A song on the radio
that was written just for you
three minutes of flying
then it was through

Deepest Hours

Whisper to me in my deepest hours
fold the night into my dreams
Something is always calling me
to close my eyes

Night rises from the shadows
with a confidence that the earth allows
The sun will quickly burn all the darkness
from the sky

A blaze of color erupts before my eyes
I have thoughts in my mind
no one can touch
yet dreams try

I call the wind to my side so that it may carry me
when I close these eyes
to touch your soul in dreams
but when I wake there will be only a trace

Just enough to hold in my heart start
this fire whispering to me in my deepest hours
telling me when it's time
to close my eyes

Mice

Lost in the haze
we fell in love
so deep inside love
never needing lessons
Desire filling the night
'til daylight
would eventually come
We would scatter
so scared of what we found
Two blind mice
       See how we run
           See how we run

Playing down despair
Dancing around broken dreams
We tried to see inside love
We couldn't see anything
in the dark
Foraging for scraps of love
Anything that might come
from inside the heart
Our senses so dulled
we lost our way
when the day was done
Blind to emotion
       See how we run
           See how we run

Love took us
over like an addiction
We crept past innocence
so quietly as to not disturb
the place
where dreams come from
We ended up lost
so lost in this maze of our own
indifference
The illusion of faith
had us drowning in our beliefs
Our hearts so blind
to what we had become
       See how we run
           See how we run

We never found our way
Couldn't see in the dark
Scattered in different directions
So afraid of love
Afraid of getting hurt
       See how we ran
           See how we ran

Ocean

Images of the ocean
       are black as night
       and deep as my dreams

My heart surveys the landscape
       tests the waters
       drowns willingly

Time Leaves a Trail

The roots that grasp the sky are the last to let go
Time leaves a trail behind like a path you traveled
... so long ago

Time will always blow us
       down the road somewhere
           like a tattered
               autumn leaf

Every heart that you touched along the way
knew you in some other lifetime
... some other yesterday

So smile at the sun
       grin at the moon
           to the wind,
               say your peace

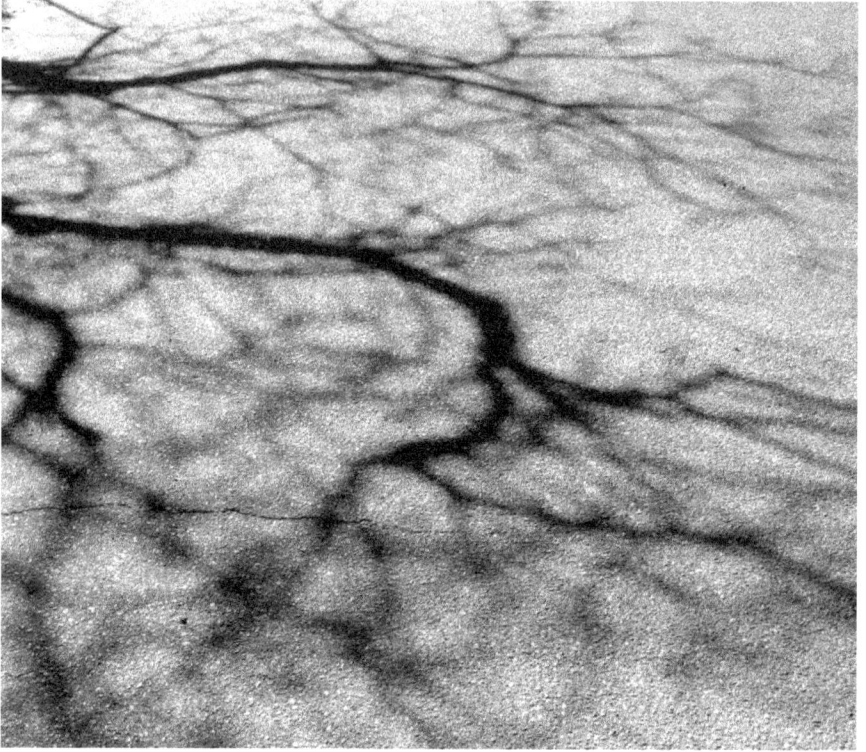

You call the wind your path because the wind never looks back

Any Resemblance

Wishing that far away could be closer
The longing in my heart is only by design
How does the heart get so lost?
I've asked myself this question
One too many times
So lost we can't turn around
So lost we can never find the same road we were on
You look like someone I used to know
That someone is gone

I used to know how to handle love
I used to know exactly what to say
You look like someone
You remind me of someone I used to know
You look like someone who's gone away

You tell me to stop using big words
That you don't understand
I said all I told you was *I love you*
Wishing that far away could be closer
You're standing right next to me
I no longer know you

I used to know how to bring you back
I used to know how to make you stay
You look like someone I used to know
You look like someone who's gone away

I used to know what to say
I used to say *I love you*

You Took the Wind at its Word

The sun fed the morning a whisper
as you sang a song into yesterday

You knew the words
you wrote them down

As you stuttered,
as you prayed
you took the wind at its word
signed with your hands to the deaf
a cross fell to the floor
so you kissed it up
to God

Honey

She calls me honey
says she's got a badass sweet tooth
My whole world is hanging from a guitar strap
electric truth

She's waiting on rock n roll
says her soul needs to be saved
I say baby, your heart has a B side
that no one has ever played

The Black of Winter

Through a wind that owns
the goldenrods
you walk backwards
into yesterday
only to find
it had disappeared
for good
for bad.

First frost
an intimate dance
of crystalline shimmer
summer a slow burn
in your memory

October crumbled
under the weight of the
waning moon
its days finalized
tortured and bent

The black of winter
arrived
to reclaim its throne
with a razorblade smile
that cut you clean through
the heart
A wound of love
like nothing
you have ever known

A backdrop of time
its arms extended
the sky so blue now
it hurts your soul
to resurrect a memory
of fallen tears
the salt within
will never let them freeze

The black of winter
betrays you once again
and the solitude of
the coming night
so cold
once again
will bring you to
your knees

Nailed

With everything set to heal
it's written in stone:
The heart will not follow
a mind all its own

You have to believe in something
The earth rotating so deliberately
You spin out of control in one direction:
Away from me

With everything set to heal
it's written in stone:
You have to dream for the things you want
or walk this earth all alone

Did you think you'd live forever
and find true love?
These are deals made in the back room of your heart
and in the heavens above

Even with your last breath
Love will be the only thing you ever needed
your head so numb by then
nothing left to feed it

I only wanted to help you heal
it's etched in stone:
Some hearts have to be taken down
all on their own

If you could only see how hard I tried
Now I'll just leave you alone

The days that you meet head on will be your only friend
I called your name from the banks of the river

Pale Moon

Pale dead moon
it comes in threes
it's hiding up there
behind the trees

Soft as water
or a kingdom of tears
pale dead moon
always disappears

Pale dead moon
shining on a shallow lake
I'm pining for a purpose
or an even break

Sweet lilac
in the breeze
broken and forlorn
I'm on my knees

Will I wish for forgiveness
or will I steal peace of mind
with the pale dead moon as my witness
my heart, my only crime

Gift Horses

I'm faded with lines that show my age
I've never looked a gift horse in the mouth
Days are dog-eared and yellowed like your favorite page
I smile, even when it all goes South

I'll never have you walk a mile in my shoes
they wouldn't fit or make you smart
One foot in front of the other you still wouldn't know
which way to start

I'm faded with lines that show my age
I've never looked a gift horse in the mouth
Days are dog-eared and yellowed like your favorite page
I smile, or try to, even when it all goes South

Drifter

You're moving on
for the sake of moving on
Leaving
for the sake of being gone

What I Mean

This town's not the same without you lately
I know you don't hate me
But by *town* I mean *my heart*

I'm chipped around the edges
and my rust is beginning to bleed through
All I'm doing is sitting here missing you

I told you so many times I don't want you back
Not much can be said for little white lies
we make our beds and then we lie back

My flag's been tattered by the winds lately
I know you don't hate me
But by *winds* I mean *regret*

Her Majesty

She tells the moon *I'll cover the tides tonight*
yes, she has that kind of pull
she stretches out her arms and pulls down
a blanket of stars
yes, she has that kind of majesty

I know that soon
all I know to be true will be right
there is never any harm in silence
when the heart is full
she tells my heart to calm
yes, she has that kind of magic
over me

She's talking to her Angels
with a tin can and a string
my love breaks off in right angles
yes, she has the strength
to bring me to my knees

She's telling all the birds up in the trees
to sing to only me
yes, she has that beautiful essence
that anything in her presence
is under her spell
is no longer free

Yes, she has that kind of magic
she has that kind of pull
over me
over me

Key

You were the Angel
who wiped the Devil's tears
and felt the thunder in his veins

You were the Angel
who taught all the others
how to spread their wings and fly

You were the Mother
who healed the wound
in Jesus' side

You were the Angel
who knew me as the only other
soul that stood under Eden's reign

You were the Angel
who held the key that opened the
door to the Universe

Angel of my heart
it was you
you just never knew

You were the Angel
who disappeared
from my life

Perched

 She pressed her lips
against the words
on the tip of my tongue
against the sentiments
that hung like a Chrysalis

All of my life I was waiting
on her kiss
to be born, to fly
as the Heart
could only dream

She pressed her lips
against the words
that were perched
on the tip of my tongue
like fledgling birds

A love by all means
meant that our souls
had touched
through many lifetimes

Yet we would only remember
this one
this one
this beautiful one

Carve

I carved a photograph out of wood
I did the best I could
It was a picture of you, the Universe, and me
I carved it with a knife made of forever
into the side of an ancient Willow tree

Baby we are the kind leading the kind and we are only
taking care of lonely

As Children

You take a streetcar to where your dreams burn
on the edges of a golden sun

You made a vow to your soul to never follow in anyone's path
You waved goodbye to me with a nervous laugh
You made a promise to the stars as if you knew them
that we would meet again someday as children

Birds float effortlessly on the updrafts of a melody
you sang once long ago

Back where time took a fork in the road
only should we meet at the other end
the song you sang came from your blessed heart

I loved you as you were

Time has a way of changing it all in the end
There is a fire that I will remember,
its warmth all encompassing
when we meet again as children

You promised to love me forever
I gave you nothing but love in trade
We are not allowed to touch where the ends of time meet
it is a silent slow parade

You took the moon's light as a sign that something shines
in any darkness we call night

I knew you could never be mine
These things are etched in the stone somewhere
somewhere that we know only as time

If there are bridges to be built from the heavens to the earth
we will be the souls working side by side to build them
with only love unbridled as the cornerstone
we will meet again someday as children

As Only a Heart

In my mind I can see you turn and smile...

dressed in only the warm sunlight from the window
a little space between the curtains
wherein a cool breeze
that time

has caressed so gently, so carefully, is allowed to blow

What we've learned is that we try
with all our might sometimes
not to get caught up
in life's undertow
to try and let
the days
just
go

In my mind I see you turning, talking to the ocean...

with one motion you leave the days you used to hurt inside
leave them all behind you, covered with the
lightest rays of the blinding sun
in the slack tide
waiting on the
pull of the
moon

Black as Silver

The moon knows where you are
even when it's only a sliver

The Angels spend lifetimes
polishing the stars

They're as black as silver
They're as black as silver

Caravan of Sighs

Flocks of birds pepper the skies
your dreams are like a Gypsy caravan of sighs
the darkness like molasses sweet and thick
the candle on the table waiting
on a single match to come into its own

Love came in like a river's fable in spring
hard and quick
overflowing the banks of your heart
always knowing its way to emotion

Flocks of birds pepper the skies
Your dreams are a Gypsy caravan of sighs
there are no words that we could speak right or wrong
that could ever do justice
to this love song

August

You sang a song into August
pressing flowers into a book of prose
if you only knew how much love it takes
      for the gates to open
      for the gates to close

Tell me hard luck stories
that always end in goodbyes
I know your heart like a promise
a promise that never lies

You sang a song into morning
as the words began to change
I know you like the back of my hand
that sounds so strange

But I understand the rain fed the river
the only way it knows how
if your love could deliver me still
like the waters I know it would somehow

You take peace as an offering
call the night your memory dark with tears
I drift on a breeze, you fall to your knees
hard as oak your tongue as you pardon your fears

Comfort me when I'm lonely
wipe my tears when I'm sad
look for reason in my eyes
      it's all we ever knew
      it's all we ever had

Embryo

If I find you somewhere in between
        my dreams and daybreak
we will not speak of this
        consider this night
        consider this fate

Consider a billion Angels holding
        light inside the sun
gathering stars together
        and placing them inside the embryo
        a gift of gratitude

Age will wrap slowly around
        the breath that you
hold so close
        consider this love
        consider this the lions share

Consider a love that
        will overpower any force in this universe
for love is the universe
        we are fragmented
        pieces of love

Hold this thought in your heart and
        reach out to make
this love whole
        consider this a blessing
        consider this your soul in the making

Consider these words all you need
       to ever know

If I find you somewhere in between
       my dreams and daybreak
we will not speak of this
       there is no need
       for our hearts have been placed

     side by side

If I find you somewhere in between
       my dreams and daybreak
we will not speak of this
       consider this night
       consider this fate

       consider this love

Wrap your heart in embers glowing...
The Crow that taps upon your window at night is all knowing

Curse

I've heard your name out in the rain
touched your blood out in the sun
I know your heart like I know a hurricane
I curse the wind that comes

Your waves never reached to kiss my shores
they came crashing in the only way they knew how
I know your heart like I know a hurricane
I can hear the winds of your soul
begin to howl

As I lean into the wind this sin cuts me clean to the bone
stops me dead in my tracks
I cannot look back
I cannot run
I know your heart like I know a hurricane
I curse the wind that comes now
I curse the wind

Only One

There's an image of a day or days
that have passed in your mind
broken down into hours
even further still into minutes

You have to believe
you need to quiet your mind
there is and always will be only one
true moment that will matter
and you are right now in it

Hand Delivered

Your panoramic heart is delivered with a vengeance
pulling out all the stops in the cog of time
I see with only peripheral visions
you cut the cord of sadness
dated and rearranged by the storm damage
you deliver only on a promise
an actor over the edge of awareness
calling out to the signs of liberty

Tomorrows all fall together as one day
oblivious to all the hate
love comes in to kiss the shore
timing is everything
you wonder how magic is performed with two hands tied
behind my back

I live with scorn
no one calls the piper
no one knows the tune
delivering only on a promise
the light fades on this side of the moon

The earth cannot turn any faster
your days are derivatives of the past
holiness was a crime you tasted
the stars all sit back and laugh
together we are so far apart
alone we are one

Look up

Time is dancing above you
it's in the form of a brilliant sun
promise the only reality divided

Innocence you believe has boarded this train
dollar signs were never the enemy
life just didn't know how to make change
delivering only on a promise
your fear has the taste of blood
in your mouth the words are shattered

Lay down your heart
here comes the flood
dog days are kept on a short leash
you wonder how long this world will spin on its own
you wash down your pills with Tangueray gin

They say the soul should always drink alone
carbon copies of days that have passed before you
you look back and see them taken by the wind
look up there is a star to catch
its only promise
to burn a hole straight through your sins

You can awaken now
dreams have delivered on a silver platter
they come back
recurring only as bits and pieces of a larger plan
you can't see the big picture now

Listen with your heart and you will hear
you've walked the road that leads to promise
forever clutching hope in both of your bloodied hands
out on the platform of time you stand now

Ends They Meet

If this road was paved with old photographs
if the tank was filled with smiles
we could go around the world on easy laughs
those smiles
would last a million miles

You and I cut a road deep as the soul
if we go to where ends they meet
it was love that led us here
Love will always lead us home

We've been talking about this trip of life so long
bring a song and your heart along
if we go to where ends they meet
the journey will be ever so sweet

Time is a Texaco map
a cup of coffee in your lap
the journey isn't about driving
it's not about arriving

If this road was paved with love
if the tank was filled with a heart's poem
we could go around the world
and Love would lead us home

I had a feeling when I first saw you that you were going my way.

Her Heart

And so she held the Sun inside her heart
the warmth of a million stars flowing
through her bloodstream

She held the Night in her cupped hands
she would come to understand
these were the strings that pulled upon his dreams

Her love was the key
Her essence could make him whole
And so she held the Sun inside her heart

She is the keeper of love
He is the gatherer of words
She held the Night in her cupped hands

He will dream in a wild obsession now
of her heart
       of the Sun
            of the love

And so she held the Seven oceans inside her heart
when she cried the Heavens opened with emotion
and the wind tore the clouds in half

He whispered don't cry, I will never tell you goodbye
it is a word our hearts will never know
And so she held all the Seven oceans penned up inside her Soul

Hours on End

Your love has turned to sunset
your heart breaks like rain
will I ever find myself
ever find myself
inside of you
again

Powerless to touch your skin now
I was Superman long ago
but dreams are days
that have passed
us by

I still love you and that's all I care to know
the love you left behind has turned
into shades of black, but your
heart's in there somewhere
keep searching
you're sure
to find
it one
day

Time will leave a mark and your love
has turned to sunset and your
heart breaks like rain
will I ever find
myself inside
of you
again

Awaken

 I woke today with thoughts in my head that
followed me here from yesterday
Time has mapped out things you once said
trying so desperately to point the way

You told me Jesus had blue eyes
I asked you how you knew what you knew
You said these things followed you here from
a time so long ago

Burning candles in your room
the only other light was the moon
brilliant shades of black was the darkness in between
you were able to walk through my dream

I woke today with a love inside of me that
followed me here from some other time and place
The peacefulness of the lines of light and shadow upon your face
a sharp contrast of things that don't last

I loved you once, maybe a thousand times, before
back where time had been born through your eyes
I love you still, through every lifetime
your soul as wild as the poetry of disguise

I woke today upon the fields with stars in reach that
followed me here from yesterday
They were meant to merely teach
I place them in your cupped hands where they will grow

You told me once that Jesus had blue eyes
I asked you know what you know
You said it came to you on the
winds of dreams

I woke today with days ahead of me, days behind me
a soul that I know as you will forever find me
we have come through time together as one
constant as the sun

I woke today with thoughts that
followed me here from yesterday
your soul beside me
always here to remind me

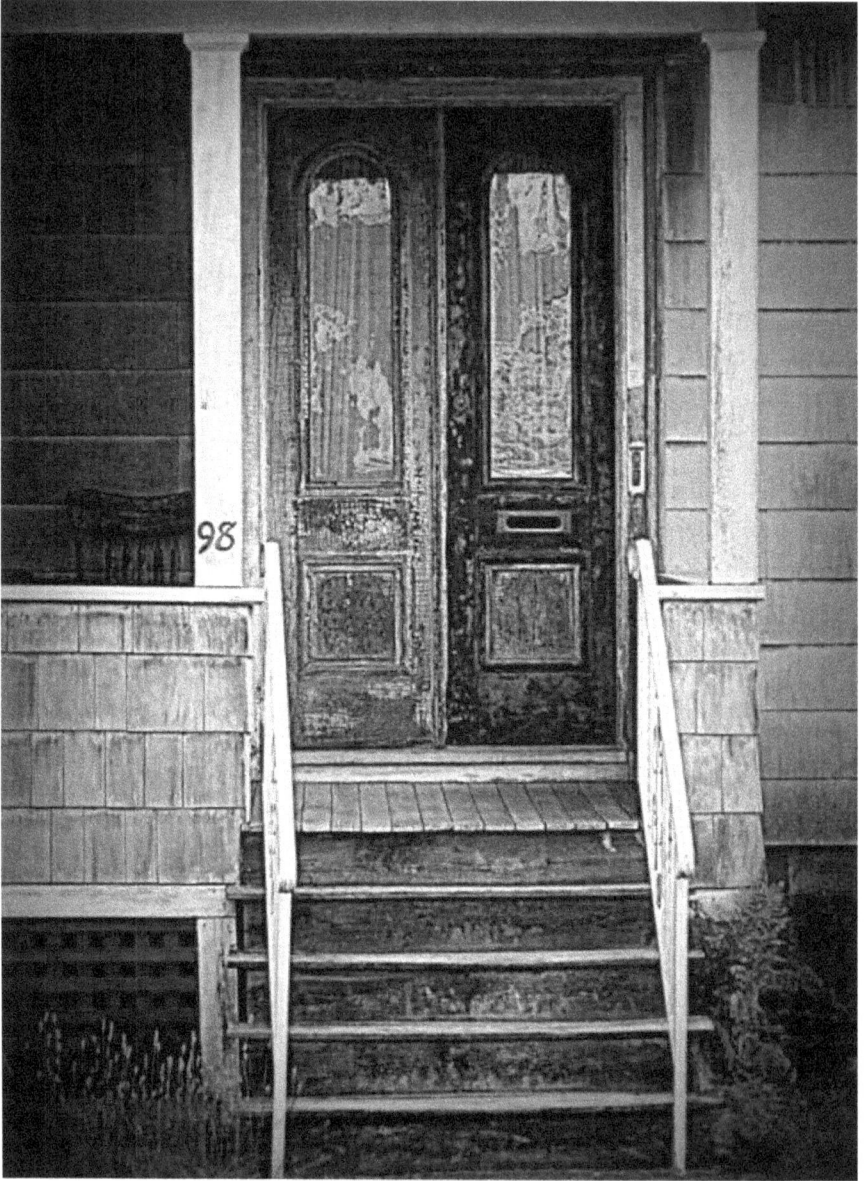

You left the door to your heart open
and someone else came in

Let Love Be

Just when I thought my heart
couldn't get any colder
the Sun tapped me
on the shoulder
Said come shine with me
just as I was about to cry
the wind came in
and asked me why?

I said it's hard to love
someone so much
when she doesn't love me
And the wind whispered softly
> *let love in*
> *let love be*

I was standing in
the beautiful silence of the Sun
feeling more alone than two
more alone than one
Everything around me
had touched you
more than once
The wind whispered softly
> *let love in*
> *let love be*

If it's love it will come back
and if it's not love
> *set it free*
> *set it free*

Blue Is

I left my peace in a place where
stars are crippled by the sun
As you speak only blue words
there is a ripple of innocence
left upon your tongue

If my ears could gauge silence I could hear
your thoughts as they gather
like the rain

I remember only things that touch
my heart
You touched my heart with
your blue words
once again

I kneel before this promise
I wait for your words to fall
like the stars
so that I may find peace in your heart
once more

Blue is the color of love
Blue are the stars above
Blue are the words that roll off
your tongue

Calm

This rain falls like a silent veil of peace
tapping upon the roof
kissing the window
calm as a baby's heartbeat

Angels turned when I called your name

Keyhole

Time came falling like darkness
through a keyhole in the Sun
a key that only Angels knew to turn

I followed the old wall that led to Banjo cat falls
I stole a lantern from the old red barn
just as the last rays of the Sun caught the tips of the leaves

Time came crawling like bitter mercy in the dark
the moon was shaped like an amethyst heart
a purple aura that surrounded both of us so gently

As angels turned the key that opened doors into love
       I lit the lantern of hope
              threw the angels a rope
                    told them climb down quietly

They whispered *We live and learn*

Blue Horses

Time on the horizon
the wind always rising to overtake
your dreams
The dawn is breaking at
the seams
Hold your head high
say goodbye to the stars
Blue Horses have brought you this far

The dust of sorrow you brush from
your shoulders
saddle your heart
its reigns
own the broken will
of a fallen soldier
You know who you are
Blue Horses have taken you this far

Blue Horses in the Red Sunrise
you ride straight into
the wind
Holding your head so high
it's been a trail
of sorrow
tomorrow
Blue Horses will lay down and die

Time is kept in a secret place
in the back of your mind
memories still show upon your face
the only Peace you find

Blue Horses you ride
changing in midstream
changing amidst dreams
as night comes in as a celestial tide
Blue Horses you ride

When the desert calls
when the stars dry up
when the oceans fall
and sagebrush blows across
the plains
the heat of the day warns you
where you are
it's been a long ride
you're weary of the stars

They shine behind a dream
so far away
will you ever see
Blue Horses have brought you this far

Now it's time to
set them free
let them run
look into the Sun
find the dream
they're waiting on you
to set them free

Cross

There's a cross made of barbed wire by the side of the road
a nest in the willow made by the crows
Does the rain bring the wind or does the wind bring the rain
We may never know
when you're a thousand miles
from where you need to go

Scarecrow bones and pay phones there's one there that's a myth
no one left to call so you blow the wind a kiss
you pass factories 'till they turn to wheat fields
time moves so slow when you're a thousand miles
from where you need to go

There's big sky ahead as the sun tears a hole in the clouds
in forgiveness you know as your soul
gasoline and coffee they both take a toll
when you're still a thousand miles
from where you need to go

Passing clotheslines and billboard signs and little country towns
the Sun is a mistress that loves to go down
motels and jail cells you've seen your share of both
Love will take the thing you needed the most
when you're a thousand miles
from where you need to go

Last to Let Go

Beautiful is the dream where you kiss the lips of paper diamonds
where you touch the silver hand of the falling rain

Now I rattle like the river in the heart of days behind you
the roots clutching the sky are the last to let go

I keep your heart inside the golden moon
and try to remember there is a bright side

that's something that only you and time
would ever know

Dream this Fire

The angels are well versed
the only pieces of time they salvage
are the roots
as they debate between heaven
and earth

Falling on the side of dreams
their consolations
nothing taken from a dream
ever meant anything
A cascade of light surrounding them
the angels are well versed in joyous revelation
as I go to sleep
so quietly they begin to sing

They will walk in between my dreams
in between the fire that burns
inside of your heart
they can do many things
but they can never
bring you back to me

Never ever finishing what they start
the angels are well versed
they know exactly
when night will fall when it will descend
as they chant a silent prayer to my soul
that this fire
that this dream
that this longing to be with you
will never end

Dance in the fire of the angels voices
they are so well versed
they are passionate
You can hear them sing as you drift off to sleep
your heart is sacrificed
you have been saved by them
one more time
as I dream this fire
that burns so deep

I take another heart down off the rack
they never seem to fit inside mine

Bluebird Road

You nailed your dreams to the stars
with a claw hammer banjo
singing a song like a bluebird in love

On the short list of things you don't know
you don't know my heart
and what I'm dreaming of

I saw a picture of you the other day
you were leaning on a sign that said
Bluebird Road

They tell me you could teach the bluebird a thing or two
I said it's nothing
I didn't already know

Bouquet

We planted seeds of unrest
and they grew into beautiful words
as the clouds flew by
like snow white birds
butterflies
and
I-don't-know-whys

Maybe I'll never know

The seeds we planted stood the test
and we watched love grow
beautiful flowers
we'll call them hours

for lack of a better word

They don't need the sun or the moon
and if we pick them too soon
they'll float on the breeze

We planted the seeds of unrest
and we grew into a poem
we stood alone
picking bouquets

of beautiful words

The train stops here, they tell you...
the train stops here

Last Leaf

Our time here on earth will be brief
Waiting on the last leaf
      to fall away

You painted a portrait of love on my soul's wall
It'll be years before time washes it away
      if ever at all

Waiting on you to say you miss me
You reach out with an apology
      instead

Tell me that you'll always love me
There was a void you say
      spiritually

Still we go only where our souls have been led
Something bigger than the both of us
      couldn't keep us apart

We spoke of many lifetimes
Got tangled in
      each other's rhymes

I'm sorry if I was wrong
I'm not sorry
      that I love you

Lead Us Home

There's no point in direction
if it doesn't lead us home
All the stars are of the sun yet there are
no shadows they have not shown

If we gave our hearts
we would have that much more to gain
in between notes and chords
there is a silence in the rain

Every heart is there to lead us home
even if it's not our own
Always remember
it was love that led us here

it is love that will lead us home

Remember and Smile

Remember me
when the Angels rock you to sleep
when you're flying
a million miles over the wild
when a broken ray of Sun points the way
remember me
when you're in the blue of the ocean deep
remember me
remember me and smile today
remember me
and smile

When the blacktop road
moves under your feet
wheels roll on for miles and miles
when you sing something soft and sweet
a song that that lasts long enough
to be a little while
remember me and smile
remember me and smile today
remember me
and smile

Smile as if the day
is the brightest thing
besides my heart
that you've ever seen
smile as if the days
that bring peace inside our hearts
are the ones
on which
we'll always lean

Remember me
when the Angels rock you to sleep
when you're flying
a million miles over the wild
when a broken ray of Sun
points the way
remember me
when you're in the blue
of the ocean deep
remember me
and smile
remember me
and smile

Tally my life on my tombstone
by the number of dogs that I have known

About The Author

Glenn Bowie is a published lyricist and photographer from the Boston area, and author of *Under the Weight of Whispers, Poem and Photographs.* *Into the Thorns and Honey* is his second book, and he donates all profits to various charities for the homeless and local animal shelters. He also owns and operates an elevator company that supplies custom-built elevators for clients from New England to Hollywood.

.

www.ingramcontent.com/pod-product-compliance
Lightning Source LLC
Chambersburg PA
CBHW020921090426
42736CB00008B/739